Losing It:
Mental Health Awareness

by
Julena Alise Wynn

All rights reserved. Without limiting the rights under copyright reserved above. No part of this book may be reproduced, stored in or introduced into a retrieval system, or transmitted, in any form, or by any means (electronic, mechanical, photocopying, recording, or otherwise), without prior written consent from both the author, and publisher Write Touch Publishing, except brief quotes used in reviews.

PUBLISHER'S NOTE:

Copyright © 2014 by Julena Alise Wynn
All Rights Reserved, including the right of reproduction in whole or in part of any form.
ISBN: 978-0692398685
Library of Congress Catalog Card Number: 2015930265

Losing It: Mental Health Awareness
Written by: Julena Alise Wynn
Edited by: Candice Abraham
Text Formation: Write Touch Publishing
Cover Design and Layout: We Read Literary Services
Printed in the United States of America

Dedication

To my mother, who sent for me when I was in New York unaware that I was suffering from a nervous breakdown.

Table of Contents

Foreward

Introduction

List of Family and Friends

Chapter One: *Leaving Las Vegas*

Chapter Two: *Around the World in Texas*

Chapter Three: *The IRS Refund Check*

Chapter Four: *Throw Away*

Chapter Five: *Return to Sender*

Chapter Six: *Group Home*

Chapter Seven: *SSI*

Las Vegas Mental Health Resources

Foreword

I had become a journalist in my junior high school years before the appearance of my mental illness. I'd written movie scripts for my mom, but didn't pursue them to the big screen. After my journey of being unaware of my mental health issues, I was diagnosed as bipolar and psychotic during the period from my late twenties to early thirties. As I become more educated on my mental illness I strive to help people become more aware of bipolar disorder. Perhaps I can help prevent the downside of not taking medication, and enlighten the public at large about living with bipolar disorder.

I began journaling when I was in the

psychiatric hospital for the second time. After being placed in a group home I was inspired by my mother, Judy Wynn, to help reveal the dark side of the disease, to show what happens when the undiagnosed go without medication. I also want families to stand by the mentally ill when the family member or friend has episodes. I've lost relationships, friendships, jobs, valuables, and condos because I was uneducated about mental illness. I did not accept the fact that I was mentally ill, and I refused to take my prescribed medication.

Introduction

There have been millions of books on mental illness. Nonetheless, mental illness is mocked on television. I began writing my life story about the transition from healthy to mentally ill. My illness was influenced by environmental stresses of friendships, relationships, and work; all took their toll on my health and this journey of bipolar disorder, and the struggle I put my family through since they were unaware of my illness.

My purpose for opening up to the world is to help stop the ridicule of the uneducated and to open peoples' eyes to the pain bipolar patients experience while traveling through the unknown.

I also want to help educate the newly-diagnosed on the importance of taking their medication and surrounding themselves with the love of family members and friends who have their best interests at heart. Unfortunately, there are some people who only want to take advantage of the assistance that the government provides for the mental ill.

Be aware of individuals wanting you to use your Medicaid card to buy them pain pills for illegal use.

Disclaimer:
Although the names in this narrative have been changed, the stories are true.

Family and Friends:

Arthur = cousin Regina's husband, now deceased

Carlos = ex-boyfriend from Puerto Rico

Charlene = Covenant of Love director

Clara = supervisor in Las Vegas job

Dad = Isaac Wynn, Jr.

Dorothy = Covenant of Love roommate

George = uncle who invited Alise to NYC

Grandma = Tabitha, a friend, unrelated

Isaac Wynn, III = oldest brother, Houston resident

Jasmine = Yesenia's sister, friend in Las Vegas

Jeremy = brother living in Houston

Jimmy = counselor at Covenant of Love

Julio = usually called "the addict", ex-boyfriend

Malia = oldest niece, sister Cheree's daughter

Maria = cousin

Mom = Judy Wynn

Quaza = cousin who was murdered on the Westside

Regina = cousin

Rose = intake person at Covenant of Love

Selena = famous Latina entertainer

Smokey = Julio's stepmom in Las Vegas

Stella = aunt

Tabitha = also called grandma, a friend

Tanya = NY cousin

Tyrone = murdered uncle

Uncle Sammy = NY uncle, Muslim religious fanatic

Yesenia = Las Vegas friend, Jasmine's sister

Chapter 1: *Leaving Las Vegas*

"Julena is so selfish," were the last words Yesenia said about me before I made up my mind that I could no longer be friends with Yesenia and her sister, Jasmine. I simply could not tolerate the lies they were telling about me.

Anger and frustration rose inside me; how dare Yesenia's sister say a thing like that about me. I felt inside I was a good friend. At times I needed my space; from time to time the feelings of exhaustion and being overwhelmed suffocated me, especially after the trip back from Puerto Rico. There I was surrounded by females nonstop without a break to rejuvenate myself.

I tried calling Jasmine to clear the air, but got no answer. I walked over to my friend

Tabitha's room to express my frustration to her; Tabitha was such a good friend that I called her "Grandma". She guided me to ignore Yesenia's remarks. On my way home I tried to follow Grandma's advice, but the anger was still there. Not being able to get the anger off my chest really put a damper on my happiness. I never liked people talking about me behind my back, which meant I would be unable to respond to them and fix things.

As life went on I kept what I wanted to say stored in my head with no outlet. I never thought of journaling my feelings; maybe that would have been a great way to really express myself. Instead I went on with life, just storing up anger every time people hurt my feelings. I didn't have it in me to tell Grandma all my deep feelings because she was the natural grandma to someone else I was dealing with at the current moment. I didn't want to be confronted every time for expressing myself on what someone did to me. But Grandma got sick and was hospitalized. I was always there with her because she was my friend who I called Grandma. I didn't want anything to happen to her when I wasn't around. I was allowed time off work to be at the hospital as Tabitha was getting better. It was scary seeing her in pain; later on she was prescribed dialysis.

Seeing her hooked up to a machine that cleans the blood wasn't a pretty sight, but I would be there with her on my lunch break and after work. I never missed a day checking up on her. Seeing the bruises from where Grandma was stuck in the arm with the needles was sad, but it was part of dialysis. There was nothing I could do to help ease Tabitha's pain of living her life depending on a machine.

I gave attention to Grandma, checking on her food supply and paying the occasional bill. She called me her granddaughter; it felt good being loved by someone who cared because I seldom heard *I love you* or other encouraging words from my own family. My mom would write letters or invite me to church, but I was attached to Grandma. We would go over Bible words for the day and attend church together when she could get time.

I wasn't spending much time with my own family; my attention was on my *other* family. They all got along and there were so many little kids; I was amused by Grandma's family. I loved how close they all were and how they could be themselves and not hide anything from their mother. I wanted my own family to be like theirs. But the calm before the storm ended with the arrival of Grandma's grandson, Julio.

November 2010, as I sat in the hospital with Grandma, I received a text from Julio. He asked if I wanted to move in around the corner from his mom's house into a house that his friend's mom was renting. I showed Grandma the text; she was happy that her grandson asked me to move in with him. Those were not her words, but that's what my brain translated to me. Julio never was a faithful young man; he had a way with the ladies, but I thought we had something more between us.

I had been his high school sweetheart. We also shared something I thought no one else had to endure at such a young age: two abortions, one at 17 and another at 21 years old. I didn't want to have the label as a female who trapped a guy fresh out of high school. In my heart I felt we were closer because of the experience, but that wasn't the case. Julio later had his first son with someone else; after that, three more would be birthed by other women.

Then came the break in our friendship, and the end of the love I had for Julio. . . . that is, once I was introduced to cocaine.

By January 2011 I realized he had a drug addiction; I was stuck in a new high rise condo with an addict who had me co-sign the lease. I didn't want to, but the pressure of moving out of my mom's home to hopefully never return was my goal. I was hoping to be denied as a co-signer by the HOA of the high rise condo company, but they approved us. I was in shock! Next I was forced to rent a television, with the assumption that Julio was going to be paying for everything since it was his idea.

Even at work I was becoming annoyed with the supervisor. Clara was placing signs up in the bathroom and making up new rules for me and others to not move around the office so much. I took it that she was targeting me because I was getting paid for days off to be with Grandma, and I had moved to a better house than she had. The frustration of being trapped inside an office from 8:00 to 5:00 pm seemed crazy, so I quit my job.

Boy, was that the greatest relief! I discussed it with Julio before I quit; I told him I was thinking about going back to dancing. However, Grandma told me if I went back to dancing she would not talk to me anymore; she meant the world to me, so I listened to her. I forgot all about what Julio and I had discussed.

That's when the stress started. Shortly after explaining that to Julio, he became mean to me and we barely spoke. He was stressing me out by asking for my part of the rent. I figured his frustration was created by my lack of paycheck; this was interfering with his ability to buy drugs.

I kept in contact with Grandma, but didn't tell her about Julio's drug addiction. God only knew what he'd do to me if he was confronted by his grandma, so his secret stayed with me. Keeping this problem to myself was stressing me out. There was no one I could talk with. I had no friends anymore and I didn't want to be judged. I was feeling trapped in a year lease that was $1,500 per month, and I was out of a job.

As months went by, I began to listen more to Grandma's advice. I let him yell or bicker about paying the rent in full and just moved at my own pace to find a new job. I expressed to my own mother that I was getting Julio back for the years I danced and he took my money; God only knew what he did with it.

Finally, in May 2012, I got a job working in the mall as a sales associate for $10.00 an hour. This was two dollars less per hour than my other job. Working in sales was a stressful position. Having a different quota to reach every day was a lot of pressure. I prayed on the way to work that I would have a great day, because there were other sales associates on the floor with me who also needed to meet a quota.

As I began to help out again with the rent I was feeling better, but Julio's drug addiction hadn't disappeared. I would get strange text messages asking for permission for him to bring some stranger into my home for sex with him. I took it as he was trying to get a reaction out of me, but I wasn't going to play into his games. I wouldn't care what he did; I had stopped sleeping with him months before, so I didn't care, and I just wanted him out. I took time out when I was off to create a calendar to determine how I could start making the full rent alone. The headaches and the 15-day notices every month taped on the door were too much. How embarrassing having my name blasted on the door for other tenants to see!

Shortly after I put my plan in motion, I gave up the big rented television that I couldn't afford. To get back on my feet someone had to be responsible. I couldn't count on a drug addict for stability, so I began saving and cutting back. Julio took his car back from me, but my mother began driving me to work to help out. I felt I was a burden to my mom, and I still had $1,500 in rent that needed to be paid.

I didn't want an eviction on my record. I eventually got evicted anyhow; on my day off Julio decided not to ask me for permission before bringing some stranger into my home and having sex on the couch. I felt heat rise in my back and began praying to God to make Julio leave. The lady at the front desk of my condo said I should just get out and break the lease.

News that my mom was planning to move to Texas to live with my brothers surprised me. I tried getting a car loan through my job, but I hadn't been there long enough. Out of frustration and stress I called up my uncle George in Brooklyn, New York and asked if I could come and stay with him. I was stressed and needed a break. I was fed up with being disrespected and harassed for my IRS tax refund by this drug addict.

When my uncle agreed to me coming to visit, I booked a ticket to New York City. I kept inside what happened to me in the condo and the fact I was escaping an addict who had lost all respect for my home. Once I was packed and moved safely across the United States, I texted the condo landlord to say that I would not be back.

As soon as my cousin, Tanya, picked me

up at LaGuardia Airport, I was taken to a house where there was a court battle going on; I was put out by my own cousin. I was still being strong; I just had to wait for Uncle George to get off and come get me to take me to his home in Bed-Stuy. Thank God I had some cash on me from my paycheck to go get my nails and one of my adopted cousin's nails done, and they showed me around Bed-Stuy until my uncle arrived. I wasn't upset; I was glad to be out of the addict's way. Nobody knew what I was holding inside. I didn't breakdown. I felt I was in control and I was going to be fine.

Later on, back on the steps where I was put out of the house, Uncle George finally appeared. Boy, was I glad to be rescued from everything! He and his girlfriend came to get me and gave me a room with a television to enjoy. I was exhausted; all I wanted to do was sleep.

Soon my uncle was trying to send me back to Las Vegas. Oh, how I wasn't ready to face anyone in Vegas. My mom was in Texas and I didn't have a car. How was I supposed to help pay rent at my mom's old house? I was so stressed that I couldn't think clearly; I was trying to focus on getting my modeling career going, but I had my uncle planning to fly me back to Las Vegas.

I didn't know what to do. I was scared of Julio finding me and taking my IRS tax refund. I reached out to Julio's stepmom, Smokey. As soon as I spoke with her I began sobbing hard; I was stuck, and didn't know what to do. I don't know if Uncle George heard me crying, but he allowed me to stay at his house in Brooklyn for another month.

Woohoo, what a relief! I was able to get something going with my dream to be a model, however, Uncle George was pressuring me about working again, this time it was bagging groceries, another job I didn't want. Later my other uncle, Sammy, called me to say he was going to help me out so I could follow my dreams, and not have to worry about the rent. Once again I felt like New York was going to be my new home.

Come December my life began to change. I had written out my goals and I followed the guidelines from Rhonda Byrne's book, *The*

Secret; I wrote it as if I lived it, and boy, did I fill up the notebook fast! I was waiting on my IRS refund check so I could fly to Puerto Rico again.

Out of the blue, in January 2012, I began dancing nonstop in my room for no reason. I began seeing things like the musical artist I was listening to. I saw a guy who wasn't there, but it was an ex-boyfriend, Carlos. I thought he did some Santeria to get me back, which meant I was experiencing witchcraft. I accepted the hallucinations as if it was just a love coming to me by magic.

I began writing a letter about me leaving the US to fly to Puerto Rico. I emailed a so-called friend the letter; he claimed he never got it. This was my letter from me and God about everything that was wrong in the world. Little did I know I was having a breakdown. The stress of not having a stable home and being in a comfortable bed was taking its toll on me. I also stopped eating meat because I didn't want to gain weight. I remember the springs in the bed that was given to me were hard, and I could feel them at night; when I would try to sleep I would take all my jackets and some clothes and place them under me so I had some comfort, but that only lasted for a few hours.

I had plans for my IRS refund check to buy a new bed set so I would get better rest, but the landlord at the new place had a very bad attitude about me for some reason. I never met him before, but he was upset and always asking for my uncle or his son. One day the landlord was talking very loudly to my Uncle Sammy about the rent not being paid. Then I realized that's why the landlord was so angry; not only was I there, but the rent was behind.

I tried not to stress more. I talked to Smokey about the situation; she told me I handled it correctly, so I smiled. I thought life was going to get a little easier for me. I was still receiving letters from the IRS about a hold-up on my check; months had passed and everyone else had gotten their IRS refund checks. I never could understand why mine was taking so long. I kept getting rejection letters from the IRS; I was becoming more and more worried.

I didn't want Julio to think I wasn't going

to pay him back for the rent he had to pay. However, it was hard to explain to him that it wasn't me, or the lady who did my taxes, it was the IRS. I thought it was taking a long time because it was my first time actually filing taxes. I remember when that last rejection letter came. I was in Brooklyn. I started crying; I was fed up with the rejection letters and I was ready to escape to Puerto Rico and start my new life.

I never got the chance to go to Puerto Rico. I suddenly began seeing things on the wall. I thought I was seeing a saint that my old friends praised named San Simon. I thought his spirit was coming for me to come back to the girls. I started seeing a heart with an X through it on the ceiling, and that scared me to the point of jumping out of bed. I would only get out of bed for oatmeal and strawberries and to light my incense for the spiritual reason of hoping better things would come.

I even thought I saw an old photo from one of my ex-boyfriends in the corner of the room. One thing stayed constant, I never stopped listening to music through the entire hallucinations. I remember leaving the brownstone where I lived and crossing the street, and then knocking on the door of a complete stranger telling her I was a psychic. She cursed me out and called the cops on me because I wouldn't leave her steps; all I could do was look in shock. I also began hearing the voices of my old boss and some family members.

The next morning I heard voices telling me to get packed; I was getting ready for Puerto Rico. I had a voice telling me to run out the house to go meet my aunty, Stella, who was a bus driver. It just so happened that a bus was actually outside, so I dashed out the house with curlers in my hair. Thank God the bus wasn't moving. I ran to the corner store, saw the bus, and went inside looking for Aunt Stella, but didn't find her. I went back to the brownstone.

I then heard another voice tell me that if I wanted to get back into the house I'd have to sing Celia Cruz's song, *La Negra Tiene Tumbao.* I began singing, and then I rang the doorbell. The upstairs tenant came down and let me in. The voice then told me to hug her, because she was

Chango from the religion Yoruba (which I had joined).

Another day when Uncle Sammy came to see me, the voices told me to hide my necklaces because he was coming to take them. I ran into the bathroom and turned on the shower as if I was going to take a shower. I ended up throwing the necklaces in the toilet, but then I was scared he was going to open the toilet and find them. I wrapped them in a towel, and then politely shook the hand of the guy my uncle brought by for me to meet. I was tired of meeting the guys from his religion. I didn't want to be bothered; I wanted to rest and just focus on modeling.

The voices started up again the next day, and I could hear my sister telling me to just leave her alone. I didn't know why I could hear her; I thought I was on the phone, and then I began to run around the corner. Next, I could hear the voice of my ex-boyfriend trying to get hold of me, to save me from the guy who told me to, "Close your eyes and wait to take a bullet to the head for the benefit of the world so it wouldn't end."

I remember running and finally stopping. I sat down on the curb and closed my eyes waiting to be killed. After I realized there was no gun shot, I opened my eyes and looked around. I didn't see any guy with a gun trying to kill me. I got up and walked back home, wondering if anyone saw what I had just done.

At that time I was not knowledgeable

about bipolar disorder; I was under the impression that someone was doing witchcraft on me to prevent me from becoming successful. I even called the IRS and told the lady handling my case that I didn't feel safe receiving my check in New York anymore. I called my mom, who sent me a plane ticket for Houston. After a few more days of the voices and hallucinations I was exhausted, but I was feeling okay after throwing away the SIM card for my cell phone. I felt this would prevent Julio, the addict back in Las Vegas, from locating me.

Before I left New York I finally felt safe enough to go to the corner store where I bought two gallons of water, one orange and some incense. I went back home and threw water all over a bookshelf and jacket that was in the room. I thought my uncle Sammy and his church people had put some type of magic oil on the jacket from their religion. After I threw the water around, I then took the incense sticks and poked them inside the orange and lit them; I placed the orange on the bookshelf and laid down, thinking I was guided to perform a cleansing ritual I had seen a lady do years ago with an orange but not with incenses. I began throwing away make-up and new clothes, shorts that were my favorite that said "Puerto Rico" on the back. I even threw away the religious necklaces. I was getting rid of clothes just like I did in Las Vegas on my escape from the addict.

I felt a heavy presence come over me

when I was sitting in the room. I thought some evil spirit was trying to get in my body, so I called my mom and asked her for a Bible verse to help me stay calm. Once I hung up I began crying again; I thought I was just grieving from all that had happened to me back in Las Vegas, but the hallucinations on the wall weren't leaving. It was like everything I saw on the Internet would pop up on the wall. When the landlord came in to check on the house I asked him if he saw anything on the wall, he said no.

Then I began thinking it was someone from across the street with a red projector shining it in my room. I didn't go back outside until my mom came to the apartment to get me, but the voices started again. It sounded like my uncle's girlfriend's sons and my cousin making fun of me. I was frustrated so I began to get upset and started walking around the corner, breathing heavily. I wanted to find them and fight. I thought they were trying to get me back because I didn't like their brother.

I came back home and sat on the wet steps and put my head down. It was as if I had an earpiece on and the phone was glued to my head, but I couldn't control it. Finally the day came when I couldn't breathe; I called my cousin Maria and I asked her if I could come over. Maria agreed; as soon as I got there I tried going to sleep. I was exhausted, but all of a sudden my breathing was bothering me again. I rushed to call 911. Maria was moving too slow for me; she began asking me questions about, was I on drugs, or had I tried something? I told her no, and asked to use her phone. My phone wasn't working because I threw my SIM card away. I was finally given a phone to call 911.

When the ambulance eventually showed up, I happy! I thought I could hear my cousin talking about me, and that's why she was taking her time to get me help. I took the phone and dialed 911 to come save me; I was living in fear of dying in my mid-twenties. Once the ambulance came I told the medic that I was having trouble breathing and something in my head popped. They seemed to be taking notes, but I didn't mention I kept seeing my ex-boyfriend. I didn't know if witchcraft had been done to bring me back, but man, I was like, this is too much. I never want to light another candle to get someone to love me.

In my mind the things I had seen from time to time with people in Santeria was truly bothering me. I kept thinking that the saint, San Simon, was trying to get me because I stopped being friends with Yesenia's sister, Jasmine, on the day of her deployment to Afghanistan.

Once we arrived at the Brooklyn hospital I kept hearing this lady from the radio in my head along with my old boss. It was as if they joined together and came up with a game show; it involved one of my ex-boyfriends and his baby's mother from Puerto Rico. They wouldn't leave me alone until I answered the questions.

The nurse interviewed me, asking what was wrong. I told her it was my breathing; I was too embarrassed to say I was seeing things and hearing voices. The nurse later told me nothing was wrong, but I knew I wasn't well . . . I felt it in my body. It felt like my body was splitting apart. I didn't remember if growing up was painful, but I was in pain. I started seeing as though I were inside a big energy ball. I didn't have a mirror to see how much weight I had lost, so I could've been underweight, and that becomes painful to the body.

Once my uncle George came to the hospital I calmed down and the voices stopped. I was watching TV in the hospital after a month of being left alone with no TV, just the music from phone in the apartment where all the voices and hallucinations started. I could focus, and was excited to get back to my mom and brothers in Houston. When my uncle and I arrived at LaGuardia I was happy, but I wanted to throw away the jacket my uncle had given me. It was a nice jacket, brand new, but when we went through the TSA check point I wanted to leave it. I kept it although there was something bothering me to leave the jacket, but I knew how security would have stopped me and asked why I was leaving the jacket? I didn't want them thinking I was a terrorist.

I tried calling my mom from the pay phone. I had lost all my contacts and the numbers I could dial because the area codes were different, so I just boarded the plane to Houston. As soon as I sat down in my assigned seat I started seeing my ex-boyfriend from Puerto Rico again, thinking, "Wow, Carlos must really be working his magic to get my attention!" With no music to help me ease my fears of flying, I kept staring at the image of my Carlos that had appeared before me a few seats up the aisle.

Chapter 2: *Around the World in Texas*

Finally I landed in Houston to live with my mom and younger brother, Jeremy. I was so relieved to be with family. I used to be afraid of going to Texas from what was seen on the news, but I was happy to see part of my family.

The voices hadn't started up again and I wasn't hallucinating the presence of my ex-boyfriend anymore. Once I had gotten the phone call from my brother, Jeremy, letting me know that I didn't have to worry about anything, I was relieved. I felt loved for the first time in a long time. Now I was going to a place where, hopefully, I had a better bed. I was away from my uncle Sammy and his religion. I could speak the way I wanted to when I answered my phone, just saying "hello" instead of "peace"; that was part of his Muslim background, and I wanted no part of it.

Soon, as we arrived in the apartment, I was given a room, and the bed wasn't anything like back in New York. It had a soft mattress and no hard springs. In my mind the addict, Julio, couldn't find me anymore, so I was feeling safe with my family. That night I got a good night's sleep; I heard no voices, but I kept seeing the saint, San Simon, on my wall. I was wondering, "Why is he following me?" I had left that part of my life behind. I wasn't going back to be friends with Yesenia's sister no matter what they are doing in Las Vegas to bring us back together.

Soon I had fallen back into a depression. Some days I didn't like doing much of anything, and then other days I had a lot of energy. I wasn't sleeping well. Once again I began thinking I was a psychic; I even had my mom take me to the Houston Library to get a psychic book by Sylvia Brown. While my mom was in the library I finally had enough of seeing Yesenia's saint; I picked up my cell phone and called Yesenia's sister. We talked for a minute; I told her the truth, that I knew everything she told Yesenia about me not being a good friend, and being selfish. Later on in the conversation I just confessed everything I was holding in. I even cried as I was confessing because I wanted to be a good friend, but I felt I had failed. This conversation took a huge stress off my chest.

Later on that day I tried reading the Sylvia Brown book, but I was once again overwhelmed by the small print. For some reason I thought I was psychic. I put the book to my forehead and rubbed the book up and down as if my mind had captured all the information. My mom wasn't the smothering type, so when I began to act out she stayed in her room. I remember the voices were entertaining me so I didn't call anyone anymore; the voices were just normal voices. Music industry celebrities and the saints from Yoruba were all communicating with me on my third eye.

I thought I had become a real spiritual

advisor! Finally I had powers to help. All the meditation had paid off in my mind. But the voice turned into that of my late uncle, Tyrone, who was murdered years ago. I have no real memories about him or the murder, but I could hear him when I would go to that bathroom and brush my teeth. I would hear him say, "That's how I used to brush my teeth." Then Uncle Tyrone's voice was saying that Isaac, my oldest brother, and I were his children; we had been left with my dad at a young age.

    I even acted out my uncle's murder; his head was cut off and placed in the microwave. I even went out of the way and wrote one of my cousins back in New York that I knew who killed our uncle. I was blaming one of Julio's baby mamas back in Las Vegas; I even blamed her for another cousin's death back in Las Vegas.

Meanwhile I continued living with my mom and my brother, Jeremy. I couldn't sleep for days. I had so much energy I would be awake for nights on end, re-enacting and hearing that people I didn't like were being arrested back in Las Vegas for doing wrong to me. When I closed my eyes, my cousin Quaza, who had been murdered, would appear with my dog, Threat, sitting on the couch at my father's house.

I was becoming comfortable with the voices and hallucinations; they were soothing to me. It seemed that God was allowing me to spend time with the cousin and uncle I had lost to death. The voices felt like I was getting a phone call, but on my third eye I felt I was so connected to the universe and closer to God. I kept seeing glimpses of saints from San Simon to the Orishas, even the KKK spirits and the Grim Reaper kept appearing. I was telling the spirits to leave the room, I wasn't ready to die.

My father, Isaac Wynn, Jr., had remarried; he and his wife were living in Palestine, Texas which is about 151 miles from Houston where my mother lives. When I was staying at my father's house I began asking him, "Who is my dad? Was I left behind because my real father was murdered?" I remember my dad laughing at me as I sat by the fireplace. I even asked my dad and my oldest brother, Isaac, for a new phone, because I didn't want to be traced by Julio, and his baby mamas in Las Vegas; they had texted me again, asking for my IRS refund check. When my brother Isaac gave me a new phone I didn't have anyone to call; I had no friends. Little did I know how attached I was growing to the voices in my head.

As soon as I returned to my mom's home the worst thing happened . . . I heard that the addict along with his family and friends were in Houston looking for me. Julio knew that my ex-boyfriend from Puerto Rico, Carlos, was also looking for me. Julio was out there with the intention of killing me. I began hearing voices that some of the people who came with him from Las Vegas were committing suicide as they were trying to find me. I remember holding my heart as if I were saving one of my friends. I began writing as if God were with me; I don't know what He thinks about me now after those letters, but He finally stopped responding to me even after so many of my "episode letters" were sent through MySpace.

The pain in my body felt like someone had a voodoo doll and was pushing needles into my back. I really began thinking someone was out to hurt me, so I wouldn't make it as a professional model. I even heard the voices of Yesenia and her sister coming to help stop the pain from the needles that Julio and one of his baby's mamas had caused. I thought my old friends had come to save me; that's why San Simon wasn't going away.

I started hearing voices that my real grandma and my friend "Grandma" were going to die soon; this continuous "news" was becoming stressful. I was thinking that whatever this gift was that God had given me was to pass on messages.

These two were hard, but I walked out of my bedroom into my mom's room and delivered the messages. At night I would see these black-looking balls flying around. They looked like demons telling me I was dead. They wouldn't let me sleep at all; I was so scared that I would get in the bed with my mother and hide under her covers. I didn't know who wanted me dead. Sometimes I would come in my mom's bedroom and tell her that someone died and walk back out. All I thought was, "Man, telling a person someone was going to be dying was a tough gift, but I guess God was blessing me with a job to spread to the world."

Galveston was the nearest beach to Houston, less than a two-hour drive. Galveston's beach was so much fun; I made it to the water. I love being at the beach; it wasn't Puerto Rico, but it was a beautiful trip with my family. We even took photos.

While on this trip, that my little brother Jeremy had planned, I was still going through the frustration of hearing my ex-boyfriend's voice. He was telling me to write ***ashe***, a Yoruba word, in the sand; after I did it he said, "You're not an Orisha." I felt embarrassed. I thought everyone in Galveston was watching me from afar; I was looking around to see who was playing a rude joke on me, but I didn't see my ex-boyfriend. We used to discuss the religion when we were together, so I believed that all the restless feelings I was going through were caused by my Carlos doing Santeria witchcraft to get me back to him.

After enjoying the beach we headed over to Joe's Crab Shack. I love eating, but the voices started as soon as we sat down. Among the family members vacationing with us at Galveston was Malia, my oldest niece and the daughter of Cheree, my sister. This time it was this famous Reggaeton artist Tego Calderon's voice telling me that Malia had been molested; he said that the guy who did it was keeping in touch with her through text messages. Every time she went to the restroom to read her texts in private I would feel disappointed that I hadn't protected her from the molester. I had no appetite, I just watched everyone else eat. I was busy listening to the voices. I didn't act out, but I was ready to go.

Heading back to Houston from Galveston was a miserable ride. I thought I was under some type of witchcraft spell that made me hear who cast the spell on me; it was like a spiritual caller ID. I felt like a wire was wrapped around my head and that's why the voices sounded so close in my ear. Meanwhile, I'm still not getting any sleep and I'm exhausted. I am not telling my mom or siblings what I'm experiencing because I didn't want to be called crazy and feel embarrassed.

Eventually the pain had worsened. The voices had me up all night; I was feeling the poking in my back and hearing that my mom was trying to kill me. I walked away from my mother's apartment as fast as I could, going in the opposite direction to another apartment complex. As soon as I got inside the complex I told the employee I met that someone was trying to kill me. I sat on the floor; the pain was intense. I thought the addict had convinced someone to do voodoo on me because he didn't get my IRS refund check. He and his baby mama were hard at work making it hard for me to rest and enjoy my money.

Shortly after I sat down in the management office the employee called the cops. When they arrived, the voices were telling me that Julio had kidnapped my ex-boyfriend, Carlos, and had him in his BMW. It just so happened there was a gray BMW outside. I began looking for where in the apartment complex they were hiding, waiting to get me. I even told the officer I was psychic; I knew who killed my uncle Tyrone. I gave the police the names of my ex-boyfriend, Carlos, and Julio and his baby mama, because those were the voices repeating in my head.

The officers were also talking to my mom, who had followed me to the other apartment complex. From the back seat of the police car I saw the names that I had given the police listed on the officers' computer screen. It said, "We got them! LOL." I didn't understand why she was laughing out loud, but I just sat in the back seat and smiled. I was saving Carlos from Julio and his baby's mama.

Finally, I was taken to a mental hospital. I kept telling the staff I was psychic, and that there was carbon dioxide in my mom's apartment and coming from my cell phone. I even told my dad that my phone was possessed; that's why I couldn't relax. The hospital staff gave me a wrist band that had my name on it; I kept telling staff members that they had my name spelled wrong. I ripped the wristband off, and sat by myself. I was looking at all these other patients thinking that there was nothing wrong with me! *They* were worse off.

I wasn't even eating. I thought eating would make them keep me in the mental hospital, so I sat staring at the TV. The voices in my head continued playing, telling me everything about people I didn't like who were also in a mental hospital. I said nothing to the doctors about the voices because I was thinking I was psychic, and it was a gift that I had to get used to because it was what all psychics went through. I still didn't know I had a problem.

I just had so much anger in me towards my mom because she left me in a mental hospital by myself. She came back with my dad and oldest brother, Isaac. Isaac was in tears, but I didn't understand why he was crying. I was happy to see them come back for me, because I felt I wasn't doing anything wrong.

Finally the nurse called me and my family into a small room and asked me questions. I felt she was being rude to me when I told her my religion was Yoruba. Later, another doctor came in to explain to my family that I was bipolar and suffering from depression. He gave me the paperwork describing my condition, but I didn't know I was depressed. I hadn't told anyone what had happened to me. For them to call me depressed was like they were reading me; I thought the staff was also psychic. The pain on top of my head was still there; I was really scared of being kept inside that mental hospital with those other crazy, loud people. I was prescribed Abilify, and I thought that would solve my problem, just take the pills and I'll be back to myself again.

Chapter 3: *The IRS Refund Check*

My oldest brother, Isaac, and I were in Dallas after I got a call from my mother; she said that my IRS refund check had finally come. She told me that the refund amount was $5,300. I thought that was wrong, so I was back to being confused. I was afraid to cash the refund check and spend the money. I saw on TV how someone could get an incorrect refund amount and have to give back everything they had spent. I called the IRS and asked for help. Even though it was explained to me, I still didn't understand a word of what the IRS agent said. I was certain that I needed to get my check fixed because I didn't want to end up in jail, so every chance I got I was calling the IRS. They no longer answered.

When I was with my dad I even told him he could have my check; I'd sign it over. Because of the pain I was in I didn't want it. I thought the check was possessed, and that's why the voices were starting again. So I would spend a little at first, and then ask for a receipt, which I kept because I wanted to be safe just in case the IRS wanted to know how and where I spent the money. I thought they refunded me too much for only working a year, but I hadn't realized that the IRS agent had combined two of the jobs I had worked . . . that's why I was getting so much back.

I wasn't taking any medication at that time, so eventually I started spending like crazy. I was shopping at the mall with this feeling that I was being guided to buy expensive Michael Kors purses, not just one, but two, starting from $300 and up. I called Yesenia and Jasmine, asking them about going to Puerto Rico and if they wanted me to buy them a gift.

In Houston, my mom my and baby brother, Jeremy, had gone shopping with me at The Galleria. I began picking out whatever I wanted, and they became upset with me. I didn't understand why. I kept saying it was my money. I wanted everything I saw. I always wanted nice skin care products and cosmetics. I saw how my oldest brother, Isaac, was able to go out and buy whatever he wanted; that's what I was going to do. I had thousands of dollars, but for some reason my family wasn't allowing me to enjoy it.

Every time I would touch the cash money I felt weird, as though the money were evil, so I began to spend even faster to get rid of it. Before I got sick with bipolar disorder I had made plans to spend the money. I even bought a thank you card for the advisor from the IRS and mailed her all my current receipts and a photograph. I have no idea if she got it, but the voices were not leaving me alone. They had calmed down and became guided voices to get around town. I had felt guided by some force to the mall and to the post office, but then I began thinking I was spiritually inclined with the angels of Texas since it was my first time in town.

I didn't spend much on food. I had no appetite. Still, I would look for wine; my mom didn't approve, but she didn't stop me from purchasing it. I would try and relax by myself. When I'd go get my nails done, as soon as I got back home I would take the nail polish off because of the celebrity voices from Puerto Rico of Tego Calderon, Yomo, and Coscuella. They were having a conversation with me through Santeria on my third eye. I was thinking I must be an important model they wanted, because they were going to great lengths to get me back to

Puerto Rico.

I remember texting Julio, back in Las Vegas, that I had finally received the check. He responded, "Where's my bread?" I ignored him because Julio felt entitled to the entire refund check. He had paid the rent when I stayed out of work for a few months. Neither my dad nor my mom took me anywhere to send him the money, so I kept on slowly spending the refund. I thought that if I spent it too fast, when it comes time to pay back all the money I spent, I could just give the receipts back and the items as an even trade so I wouldn't go to jail for the incorrect check.

When I was in Dallas with my brother I tried booking my flight to Puerto Rico. However, he said I didn't have any money left, and he wasn't taking me to the airport. I remember giving this so-called psychic lady over $400 because she said there was something a family had done to me that was black magic, and that's why I was going through so much. I wanted peace. I wanted to sleep again, and for the hallucinations to stop. I never told my mother what I was doing; boy, do I wish I would have or could have saved that money. But when you're in the moment and it's scary, you want to fix the problem of the horrible witchcraft that you believe is harming you.

Once I was flat broke from all the wild spending and not thinking clearly, my oldest brother, Isaac, had suffered enough of my outbursts. I was worsening and I was calling Jasmine frequently because I thought her saint was really doing his job to keep whatever wish they had made. I remember calling her and trying to have a real conversation about guys and cosmetics, but the voices were in the background. This time I thought it was the guy I had written the letter about God to, and I could hear his voice saying, "Aww, that's so cute, they're speaking again." I ended the call fast because I was getting bored being on the phone with her, and I really didn't want to talk to her after all the stuff she said about me. Since I had the voices and was seeing San Simon on my wall, I figured it would pass. I was getting annoyed and frustrated with it all, and then I started accusing Jasmine of doing stuff to my brain. I accused her of having a doll with wire wrapped around it to get me back for not being a good friend. She laughed, but I didn't see anything funny. I even texted her, saying it was Tego Calderon because on Twitter his page he approved her as his friend to follow me. So I thought Tego Calderon was using Santeria to keep in contact with me for modeling business.

Chapter 4: *Throw Away*

My father and step mother invited me to live with them in Palestine. I was still off my medicine and having hallucinations big time. I was seeing a famous Puerto Rican DJ, music artists, and the globe of the world . . . all playing out like a movie of what the future was going to be. I thought I was having premonitions, but a black arm would come down and scare me and the voices would say, "Go spend time with your father!" When I heard this command it would scare me so much that I would run into the living room where my father was watching TV.

I listened to the voice; I thought God was spending quality time with me, and this is what a spiritual journey felt like. After a while I began taking baths with seasoned salts because the voices were making me think it had been a while since getting a spiritual cleansing for the New Year. Since I was thinking I was psychic, I had the power to do so. Soon after the baths I began throwing away my expensive cosmetics; my dad would go back and retrieve the make-up, products like Christian Dior lip glosses, but I would say, "I know what I'm doing." Honestly, I wish my dad would have placed the items out of my sight for when I came back down from the whirlwind.

According to the Houston doctors who diagnosed me, I was dealing with bipolar depression. In Houston, after spending all my money, I took a beautiful watch that was given to me for Christmas and pawned it. I also pawned my name plate for $150.00; as a teenager I had begged my mother for this plate. Next I went to a nice Mexican restaurant to eat by myself because my family was being mean to me, and I didn't know why.

That night I was sitting in the bedroom at mom and Jeremy's house, going through all the clothes that I had worn around Julio. I started placing them in a trash bag; they were all worn once, clothes that I had purchased in Las Vegas from when I worked at the mall; dresses I had seen in the window that I saved up for to buy, a long sleeveless flowing beautiful turquoise summer dress, and lots of pants. I even gathered the high heels that I had worn around him when we had the high rise condo together. Everything went into the bag, even the jacket that my Uncle Sammy gave me before I left Brooklyn; I thought he had put a chip in the lining that would track me down should I tell what I had seen.

Sammy's religious group had this school which they held for some kids. I didn't like being at the school, or hearing the men call themselves God. I went downstairs to the dumpsters and tossed in all the bags. I felt as if someone was going to pop out the dumpster, so I ran as fast as

I could back into the house to avoid being captured. I didn't tell anyone what I was doing, because I wanted this restless feeling to leave me alone.

    I kept thinking that Julio, or someone who didn't like me, wanted me to lose everything and start over in life; their wish was coming true because this evil feeling spirit wasn't leaving me alone with its powerful, indescribable force over my body. Nonetheless, I was holding on to the celebrity voices because I thought that was something all celebrities go through. That's why, once they make it, they only are seen with other celebrities. Soon after coming back inside from throwing most of my belongings away, my younger brother Jeremy was on the phone with my dad, saying: "Yeah, she's doing it again." I didn't know what he meant by it, so I went straight to my room. Every time I threw things away I would feel like the problem was going away with my belongings. Each time the problem left, but it would come back.

My oldest brother Isaac let me move in with him in Dallas. I was broke, but I began throwing away more jewelry; the jewelry had been gifts, but I didn't keep it because I wasn't friends with the givers anymore. I was getting rid of memories and whatever evil spirits that followed with the jewelry. I wanted no more to do with witchcraft. I wanted to sleep, and be at peace, so I could get my modeling career going.

I was going to the trash shoot to throw

away all gold bracelets because the hallucinations were following me again, and I was tired of seeing Yesenia's saint in the air. Once again I thought Yesenia and Jasmine were in Las Vegas doing black magic, getting aroused about the fact I was losing my mind. They were getting phone calls from me talking crazy, because I wasn't there for Jasmine's deployment party before she was shipped to Afghanistan. I began opening up to my mom about all the crazy stuff I had seen while being friends with Yesenia's family, acts involving jars and cigars and Brandy liquor.

Chapter 5: *Return to Sender*

My oldest brother Isaac had endured enough of my undiagnosed mental episodes in Dallas. My mom had returned to Las Vegas to live, so I was sent back to Vegas to stay with my mom. I'm guessing she left Texas due to my episodes of anger outbursts and profanity toward my family members. I had been told that I was going back to Las Vegas and that mom would be picking me up at McCarran Airport. Knowing she was there waiting for me helped. I wasn't scared like before when my Uncle Sammy tried to put the voices in my head.

I thought I was being sent back to Las Vegas because being on my spiritual journey meant to come back and confront every person who ever talked bad about me, disrespected me, or thought I was a punk. The voices and hallucinations of Uncle Tyrone and Quaza, who were both murdered, returned to me. I thought God allowed me to see them and hear their voices to know that it was time to show these people who hurt and disrespected me that I was ready to speak up and fight anyone ready to feel the wrath of Julena Alise, the not-so-nice-anymore Julena Alise.

When I got home I was broke; all my tax

refund money was gone. All I had were some clothes and a pair of the Jessica Simpson heels. I had thrown away most of my lounging clothes. I just so happened to have a bucket that had some left-behind clothes. After being picked up from McCarran Airport by my mom I was doing ok. I was restless on the plane ride back from Dallas; I don't know if I scared anyone on the plane. I had the group *Plan B* singing "No Secreto" in my head to ease the fear of flying alone.

Shortly after landing I was happy to be safely on the ground. I rushed to get my luggage and get home to mom's house before anyone recognized me and told Julio. In the car with mom, I sat in the back seat just observing the casinos and not saying anything; I thought that finally I was going to get back to sleeping well. The peace lasted for a short second. I wanted to get on Facebook and announce that I was back in Las Vegas. I planned to get back into the Latin nightlife and start over, but be away from the addict. Should Julio appear, I was going to face him; whatever happened I was going to show him that I wasn't going to be bullied anymore.

I had no computer, so I knocked on my niece's bedroom door and asked to use her cell phone. She said ok, but once I mentioned Facebook she jumped up out of her bed and tried snatching her phone back. It set me off that she was disrespecting me, and that wasn't a good thing. I was back to not allowing anyone to run over me, but then it led to a fight. I remember my mother separating us because I was seeing red; they locked me out the house and called the cops on me. I was later told to put some clothes on and leave with the officer. I did because I didn't want to go to prison for fighting with an underage child, but I was thinking that she knew at least to never disrespect me and I was happy with that.

Shortly after I got dressed and came out of my room to the officers, an ambulance came and took me to Centennial Hospital. They put me on a suicide watch unit and I didn't understand why I was there. I loved my life; I was tired of feeling like I was fighting to live. The nurse came, took my blood, and had me change clothes. In my mind I was wondering if Tabitha was back in the hospital; I didn't have my friend to talk to about what I was going through. I just laid in the hospital bed and went to sleep for a quick moment, then popped back up wondering when I was going home. Another ambulance crew brought a gurney with restraining straps on it; I politely got on it, not knowing where they were taking me or why. I thought I was getting placed in a hospital room, but they took me out the hospital. As I watched out the ambulance window I was memorizing areas so I could call for help once I could get to a phone. They arrived at their destination: Rawson-Neal Psychiatric Hospital.

    I was scared every second. I didn't know if I had been placed in jail, because only the nurses could activate the doors to open and close. I began having hallucinations of guys' heads being chopped off; I thought God was releasing His chosen back to earth after their spiritual journey, but I still never got why I was being kept in this place. I held in my fear and looked forward to going back home soon, as soon as the police were finished with whatever my family was reporting on their witness reports.

July 2, 2012 was my birthday. I was stuck in the Rawson-Neal Psychiatric Hospital being observed by different people, but not really aware of what my family said to the police. I was just looking forward to getting out of there; it felt like I was in a prison even though I had never been to a prison or jail before. The feeling of not being able to leave on my own was bothering me. Meanwhile, mom came to visit me and brought me clothes once she realized I was still wearing the same outfit that I had worn when the ambulance picked me up. Day after day nurses and staff gave out snacks and medicines, watching us swallow every pill.

    At least for breakfast, lunch, and dinner we were allowed to leave the main waiting observation room; I always sat by myself because I never really made friends easily, especially with total strangers. Finally, after talking with three different doctors at the same time, they allowed me to go home with my mom. The doctors never explained to me why I was being held in the hospital, which made me say "Yes" to everything they were asking just to get released back to my family.

I took the prescribed medicine. Once again the voices had me thinking I was going to be picked up and taken to Puerto Rico where I could start my new life. The only way I could go was to take the meds, but each day was a struggle; no one that I was writing in Puerto Rico was appearing to take me. I was reaching out to DJ Warner, thinking he and I were going to be together. I felt I was a very attractive person who could have any guy I wanted, but I couldn't stop writing him.

That indescribable powerful force was coming back again like when I wrote the letter to a so-called friend about God. Every day that went by I emailed DJ Warner from my mom's phone, hoping to get a response. As an activity, my mom would take me to the library. I would check out music and read one book that was about Selena, a famous Tejano singer who was murdered; that was the only book I chose. The CD I selected would play on repeat, and I sang along at the top of my lungs.

Next I changed the music to Hector Lavoe, another famous Puerto Rican salsa singer, who passed from drugs. I stopped taking my medicine thinking I could live pill-free, but I had no clue about being diagnosed bipolar until the second time having the cops called on me. While I was sleeping, my mom told the police that I had threatened her with a butcher knife. I had been sleeping after watching the election of the new pope; I woke up to a police woman telling me to shut up. I didn't know what I did this time; each time the police showed up I was clueless.

Here we go again, back to Centennial Hospital where I used to stay at Tabitha's side when she got sick. Again I was placed on suicide watch, again the nurse drew my blood, again they were feeding me. I guess that was supposed to comfort me, but I couldn't sleep. I was still up and restless for what felt like an eternity. When I saw the ambulance attendants come again with their gurney and straps, I knew I wasn't going back home. I didn't know what I had done this time, but the voices about missing out on the trip to Puerto Rico were repeating in my head . . .

everyone who knows me also knows how much I love Puerto Rico.

    Returning to Rawson-Neal Psychiatric Hospital for the second time, I wasn't as scared as before, but this time I thought Rawson-Neal was just a jail that served my area of town. That's why I was there, because my mom was tired of arguing with me and telling me to get a job or to get out her house. She demanded I leave even though every day I would wake up and watch *Un Nuevo Dia,* then walk three to four miles to our local library just to get out the house; as I look back it shocks me that I was able to walk that far. I was hallucinating the entire way to the library, but I was at peace being by myself. I would take off the jacket I was wearing, or the book I was carrying, and drop it, but keep heading to the library no matter how far it was on foot.

I even pawned my favorite Michael Kors handbag, which had cost almost $800, for only $20 just to get coffee and something to eat because I wasn't getting much help from my family. They thought I was just being a mean person who had lost respect for everyone. Each stay in Rawson-Neal lasted almost a month, but this time my mom didn't come and visit me or bring me clothes. I felt abandoned, as if all my family had thrown me away. I began to write, and I began thinking it was not nice that I was going to be left in Rawson-Neal forever. Then my doctor advised me about a group home called

Covenant of Love that was willing to take me in and help me get on my feet. I agreed, because I had no family. In my mind I felt that I had blown it with my family due to the repeating episodes of erratic behavior. My mom told me that even my brother and father were unable to tolerate me because of the unpredictable episodes that had occurred during my visits with them.

Chapter 6: *Group Home*

Because I hadn't been taking my meds I was being sent to Covenant of Love, a group home in Las Vegas that would assist with my bipolar disorder. That wasn't explained to me; I was released from the hospital with the clothes on my back and all the papers I had used writing. As I read the diagnosis I saw where it stated that I couldn't work for a year.

The lady who was transporting a group of

us from Rawson-Neal, Rose, took us to the group home for our intake interview. She made sure that we had all our paperwork. This was the first time I had seen my diagnosis from my original stay with Rawson-Neal; that time I had been released to my mother with only a prescription. As I arrived at the house where we were to do intake, I immediately disliked the neighborhood. It was what I would call "in the ghetto", what is known in Las Vegas as "the historic Westside". Why wasn't this explained to me?

I guess when you don't have family support you have to deal with what is in front of you in that current moment. I was scared, because I had no one. I would call my mom in anger, thinking she had done this to me. I couldn't understand why she had not wanted me back when I was released. Why she was so mean to me?

I had no one in my corner. I didn't have Grandma anymore; I was too embarrassed to call her again after leaving a voicemail on her daughter's phone. I was upset that she didn't answer when I called. I only intended to check up on Grandma and the little boy I had grown to love as my godson. I had forgotten all about the refund, so I didn't know if Julio, the addict, had demanded that his family stop talking to me. I felt that I had lost my Grandma.

The first night at the Covenant of Love we were taken to a group meeting. Dorothy, my roommate from Rawson-Neal, and I attended. I was asked to introduce myself and tell a little about myself. I remember talking about wanting to save my cousin from prison. If only I could get cocaine as a pill, maybe that would save lives and get some people's sentences lowered. It sounds crazy now, but I thought that if I could get a doctoral degree to become an analyst I would be able to get this powder turned into a pill which could be sold over the counter so people wouldn't overdose anymore.

One of the girls who had been in the group home for some time asked if I was a cop. I don't know why, but I politely said, "No", and finally I was able to sit down. The CEO of the group home didn't judge me or laugh, so I didn't feel stupid for telling the truth. I was still in shock that Julio had perched on my bathtub edge and admitted to me that he had almost OD'd . . . and laughed! It scared me, because what if he had OD'd? Then I would've had to explain to his grandmother, son, and daughter what happened; that was stressful and scary to think about. Several days after moving into Covenant of Love, a short guy named Jimmy came over and sat down to talked with me. I thought I was in a program that my mom had set up; she expected me to participate in the program so I could go back home. I began to cooperate and have the one-on-one sessions with Jimmy, the therapist; slowly I began to open up to him. However, I talked more openly with my roommate, Dorothy. I never asked her what her diagnosis was, I just accepted her. She was cool. On our first day out of Rawson-Neal, Dorothy bought McDonald's for several of us; she was very motherly. She would surprise me with clothes, shoes, or lotion. She would even take me out to grocery shop and ride with her to the mall so I didn't feel so down. It depressed me to be in a place that was not my mom's house, a big house. Instead I was living in a little house on the Westside of Las Vegas; in my prior life I would never have been there, especially after last seeing my cousin Quaza alive in that area. I couldn't understand why I felt like I had lost everything. I had scared everyone away from me by sending out letters. God only knows how the receivers took my crazy emails and mail.

All I know is that living in a three-bedroom home with six other roommates meant I still wasn't sleeping like I had back in 2009. One of my roommates and I would have disputes about my waking up at 4:00am. I was still, in my mind, back in Las Vegas but with the attitude of not allowing anyone to disrespect me, and I was still holding on to all the voices and hallucinations I had of my uncle and cousin. I continued waking up whenever my body would rise.

I was always writing to keep my mind off being in the group home. Some days I would walk to the library wondering why I was brought back to that same side of town where my cousin was killed. I kept on going though; it was better than being stuck in a small home with people I didn't know, and probably wouldn't have befriended in a different situation. I had to face the music, so I created another Facebook page to get my life back to where it used to be before I moved in with Julio.

Having no car and Dorothy being the only one with a vehicle was tough. Whenever she wasn't at the gym or working, we'd go shopping. Sometimes we would go up to the main office of Covenant of Love where Charlene, the CEO, was working and talk for a brief moment. I ended up liking some of the staff; Rose was my favorite. We both liked royal blue. She had the commanding presence I had always wanted. When you met Rose you knew she was a strong woman who didn't let anyone talk crazy or disrespect her. I began to believe that God and my cousin Quaza were guiding me to overcome the hurt of his passing. I was meant to tighten up and be like him, no pushover. I had so many hallucinations of Quaza and God that I was always thinking I was going to die on this spiritual journey.

Every Sunday I went to a Mormon or Catholic Church with Dorothy or another roommate to get out of the house and clear my head from all the loneliness and sadness of not having my family come and get me. Sadly, after being in the group home dealing with so much about death, my cousin-in-law had passed on Memorial Day, while I was at the Puerto Rican Festival. It was a shock that when I was having hallucinations and hearing voices I heard my cousin Regina arguing with Arthur. I never said anything to anyone. I regretted keeping silent; maybe speaking up would've done something, but I had stopped passing messages on to my mom. I didn't like the so-called gift that I thought God had given me.

Talking to Jimmy and Rose almost every day was great. They didn't come around only to make us take are meds; they treated us like human beings. I remember Rose's words to me: "Don't let anyone make you do anything that you don't want to do!" I felt loved. I tried finding Rose on Facebook, but no luck. I reminded myself that all good things must come to an end. People are in our lives for a season or a reason.

When I got the approval to move out of the group home and move in with my dad's oldest daughter, I was so happy. I was getting away from those roommates I knew nothing about; I hadn't been there to make friends. I wanted to get back to my family; I was getting better due to the staff coming by to refill my meds and check up on me. It was my birthday again, July 2, 2013. I spent it in the group home, but my mom took me out to eat with my dad because the A/C had gone out. I was thrilled to get out of that small, hot house.

Chapter 7: *SSI*

The day had finally come. I was moving out of Covenant of Love, the group home that I had shared with six other people. Dad's oldest daughter, Selena, was allowing me to stay with her; after months of begging my mother to take me back, but to no avail, I had found another outlet. I didn't say a proper goodbye to the staff because I have never been good at saying goodbye.

Off I went on July 3, 2013; I wasn't looking back. God had answered my prayers by getting me out of that hot house. Nobody should ever have to be that miserable. I had one box and my journal; the writings that I had begun in Rawson-Neal meant everything to me. Writing was my outlet for expressing my true feelings instead of keeping them stored in my head. Finally, I was able to relax. I was thinking I was in a better place. I didn't know much about Selena, but I trusted her. I felt it was time for me to get along with unfamiliar relatives; she was taking me in after all I had put my family through.

As soon as I had dropped my box and bags at my new home, I felt grateful to be away from those roommates. I wanted to get my life back, but I was still out of work. My only income was a government food card called EBT. Being depressed caused me to gain weight because I was eating a lot and picking up bad eating and drinking habits. I thought by drinking diet sodas I would stop gaining weight, but I was also baking chocolate cakes and eating a whole one myself.

I was missing my real family. I wanted to be with my mom again; I missed her, but I had to wait. Mom had texted me to say she was waiting for God to speak to her heart. Days had passed, and Selena approached me about an appointment at the Social Security Office; she wanted me to apply for disability payments (SSI) based on my bipolar disorder diagnosis. Since I wasn't living with my mom, I had only two choices for a home at that time, my dad or his daughter, Selena. My dad didn't live in Las Vegas, so I chose his daughter.

She never showed me any mail that would come for me from the Social Security Office. For months I was unaware that I had SSI money coming to me. I trusted her and never thought anything wrong about her. Selena didn't work, which was odd, but I never questioned how she paid the rent. She was nice too; she would do my hair and give me clothes she didn't wear anymore. Sometimes she'd give me something new, but most of the time it was hand-me-downs. I thought Selena was giving me the hand-me-downs because I had gained weight and she was being a big sister.

Things started changing in December. Both mom and my brother were asking me how much money SSI was sending me each month. I didn't know; I had the case worker from the welfare department tell me over and over again that I had money. I had SSI, so Nevada was cutting down the amount from my EBT card because I was already receiving enough money. I was supposed to be receiving an allowance of $30 from Selena, and I explained that to my case worker, so I still didn't understand the money issues. Things weren't feeling right, my gut wasn't settled.

On January 13, 2014, after my family's concerns about my SSI surfaced, my mom wanted me to come back home. Boy, was I happy! Finally God had spoken to her, so I packed my bags, more than ready to get back to where I called home. Even my dad and brothers were involved in helping me get back home to safety. I felt loved again. My mom was hearing good things from my dad. He told her about his observations of my recovery from the Thanksgiving trip I took with him and my stepmom. I had no voices or hallucinations, no feelings like I was being watched or traced. I was at peace, enjoying the family time with my dad on better terms. I even felt closer to my dad and stepmom; all the delusional talk was over. My mental health doctor, Dr. Peter T. Pinto, had placed me on the best medicine before I left for my vacation, called Latuda. It was a drug used to treat bipolar depression in adults. I even began to lose weight again. The Seroquel, a different depression drug that I had been using, was making me gain weight rapidly. I was getting frustrated again. I was supposed to be a model and my dreams were being hindered.

Once I was back home with my mom and settled in, she showed me the mail that had come from the Social Security Office. After going to change the payee to my mom, things were moving up. I wasn't feeling stressed; I began sleeping good again, going to the library, working out, eating right, listening to good Spanish music, singing, not arguing, going to church, cooking, and talking more to my dad and brothers.

Some days I feel my baby brother James doesn't really like me after what he experienced in Houston. Back then I thought there were spies in the air vents and I placed cardboard over them; I think I unplugged the TV and James' Xbox. Facing the people I offended when I didn't have my proper medicine is hard, but I work through it. I talk to my mom every day, so we keep the communication open. I have had no more episodes. I miss not having all my family together, but, with the therapy I'm waiting for through Medicaid, I look forward to being able to continue to cope with the bipolar disorder.

Las Vegas Mental Health Resources

Rawson Neal Psychiatric Hospital:
1650 Community College Dr., Las Vegas, NV 89146 (702) 486-4400

Covenant of Love Behavioral Services:
1100 N. Martin Luther King Blvd., Las Vegas, NV 89106 (702) 255-7733

Southern Nevada Adult Mental Health Services:
6161 West Charleston Blvd., Las Vegas, NV 89146 (702) 486-6000

Clark County Social Service Community Resource Center:
2432 N. Martin Luther King Blvd., Suite D, North Las Vegas, NV 89032 (702) 455-4270

Division of Welfare and Supportive Services:
dwss.nv.gov

Social Security Administration:
4340 Simmons St, North Las Vegas, NV 89032 (702) 646-0861

Exodus Family and Guidance Services, LLC:
Dr. Karen D. Lee (702) 466-4360

www.ingramcontent.com/pod-product-compliance
Lightning Source LLC
LaVergne TN
LVHW021400080426
835508LV00020B/2379